JOHN CORIGLIANO

TROUBADOURS
(VARIATIONS FOR GUITAR AND CHAMBER ORCHESTRA)

GUITAR AND PIANO REDUCTION

ED 4204
First Printing: August 2008

ISBN: 978-0-634-08910-7

G. SCHIRMER, *Inc.*

DISTRIBUTED BY
HAL•LEONARD®
CORPORATION
7777 W. BLUEMOUND RD. P.O. BOX 13819 MILWAUKEE, WI 53213

Composer's Note

For me, the compositional process starts well before the generation of actual musical ideas. *Troubadours* began with guitarist Sharon Isbin in the early 1980's. At that time, she asked if I would write her a concerto, and I was decidedly lukewarm about the idea. The challenges of writing for a highly idiomatic instrument that I didn't fully understand were augmented by my dislike of most "idiomatic" guitar music, as well as my fear of writing a concerto for an inherently delicate instrument.

But Sharon persisted. She sent me scores, tapes, and letters with ideas on the kind of concerto it could be. When I received a letter from her with articles about the age of the troubadours, and particularly some celebrated women troubadours, I started thinking about the idea of serenading and of song. Slowly the conception of a troubadour concerto began to form.

During this process the crystallization of what I love most about the guitar took place: It is an instrument that has always been used to speak directly to an audience. Lyrical, direct, and introspective, it has a natural innocence about it that has attracted amateurs and professionals, young and old.

It is very hard to preserve this sense of innocence in the music world we live in. Performers are held to razor-sharp recording standards as they compete with each other for superstardom. Composers have such arsenals of techniques from the past, present, and other cultures, that the idea of true simplicity (in contrast to chic simple-mindedness) is mistrusted and scorned. So the idea of a guitar concerto was, for me, like a nostalgic return to all the feelings I had when I started composing—before the commissions and deadlines and reviews. A time when discovery and optimistic enthusiasm ruled my senses.

Therefore, *Troubadours* is a lyrical concerto. It does not "storm the heavens," and its type of virtuosity is quite different from that of my other concertos. By writing for chamber orchestra, with some of the instruments placed offstage, I was able to achieve the balance I desired between soloist and orchestra.

"Troubadour" was the name given to the poet-musicians of southern France whose art flourished from the end of the 11th until the end of the 13th century. While this work utilizes some of the flavor of that time in the solo writing and percussion, it is more concerned with the idea of the troubadour rather than a display of early techniques.

The concerto is a series of free variations on an original troubadour-like melody. The last phrase of this melody, however, is an actual quote of the final phrase of the song "A chantar" by La Comtessa (Beatritz) de Dia (late 12th century). *Troubadours* is in three parts, with a cadenza separating the second and third parts. The outer sections are slow, the central one fast. The main theme resembles many troubadour tunes in that it is basically stepwise and revolves around two tonal centers, each a step apart. This stepwise descending melody forms the building blocks of seven chromatic chords that run through the work. These chords first appear in string harmonics, fading in and out of nothingness.

They soon dissolve into each other as a background for a series of descending lines in the oboe, violins, clarinets, and flutes. These variants of the troubadour tune float slowly downward surrounded by the cloudy chords. The solo guitar fades in and out with fragments of its theme, as if from a distance. The downward lines finally disappear, and the soloist is left alone to play the central troubadour theme. The orchestra slowly joins the soloist in lyrical variations as the cloudy harmonies return.

The second section is announced by an offstage percussionist. (One of the two onstage players has gone backstage to join an oboe and two bassoons.) This trio of double-reeds and drums acts as a raucous shawm band. (Shawms were ancestors of oboes and bassoons—much reedier and coarser than today's refined instruments.) The band interrupts the onstage soloist and orchestra in a series of multiple conversations, and as they reach a peak, two offstage French horns add to the interplay. This cacophonous climax is followed by an extended solo cadenza in which the guitarist changes the mood from boisterous to intimate. At the very end of the cadenza, the guitar introduces a slow, ornamented variation of the troubadour tune accompanied by a simple chaconne-like seven-chord progression, again derived from the descending note pattern of the theme. This pattern repeats as the orchestra slowly joins the soloist, but the seven-note chaconne progression begins to change into the original chromatic cloud-chords as the more abstract descending variations of oboe, clarinets, violins, and flutes float downward and the opening textures return. This slow change from the innocent harmonies and lines that started at the end of the cadenza to the more abstract, hazy filigrees and sonorities that opened the work is possible only because they are generated from the same ingredients. The change is not one of material or technique, but one of attitude. The innocence of the earlier chaconne is gone, replaced by another kind of expression. The loss of one is balanced by another.

Troubadours ends as it began, in clouds of memory.

— John Corigliano
(1993)

Performance Note

If using wireless sound reinforcement, the soloist has the option of entering and exiting from backstage. Begin performance backstage and walk slowly onstage after the opening notes of the run in measure 38. Sit in soloist's chair by fourth cue in measure 40, before tag. At measure 294, walk toward backstage while playing. Measures 309 through the end are performed backstage.

With special thanks to Scott Wilkinson for his assistance.

—Sharon Isbin

"Troubadours" was commissioned by the Saint Paul Chamber Orchestra,
The Concordia Orchestra, and the Phoenix Symphony for guitarist Sharon Isbin,
with funds provided by the Meet the Composer/Reader's Digest Commissioning Program
with additional support from the Mahadh Foundation.

The world premiere was given October 8, 1993 by Sharon Isbin
with the Saint Paul Chamber Orchestra, Hugh Wolff conducting,
at the Ordway Music Theatre, St. Paul, Minnesota.

A recording by Sharon Isbin with the Saint Paul Chamber Orchestra,
Hugh Wolff conducting, is available on Angel Records/EMI 72435-67672-25
"American Landscapes."

Instrumentation:

<u>Onstage Ensemble</u>
2 Flutes (2nd doubling Piccolo)
Oboe (doubling English Horn)
2 Clarinets in B flat (2nd doubling Bass Clarinet)
2 Percussion
Piano (optional)
Strings (minimum players 6.6.4.4.2)

<u>Offstage players</u>
Oboe
2 Bassoons
2 Horns in F

Duration ca. 23 minutes

Performance material is available on rental from the Publisher:
G. Schirmer/AMP Rental and Performance Department
P.O. Box 572
Chester, NY 10918
phone 845-469-4699
fax 845-469-7544
www.schirmer.com

Information on John Corigliano and his works is available at www.schirmer.com

for Sharon Isbin

TROUBADOURS
(Variations for Guitar and Chamber Orchestra)

John Corigliano

piano reduction by Erik Nielsen

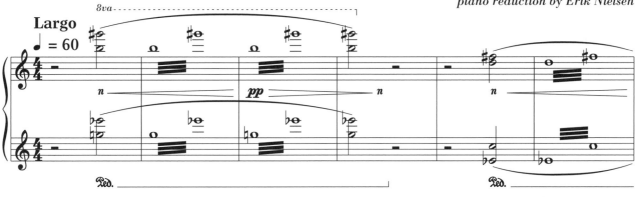

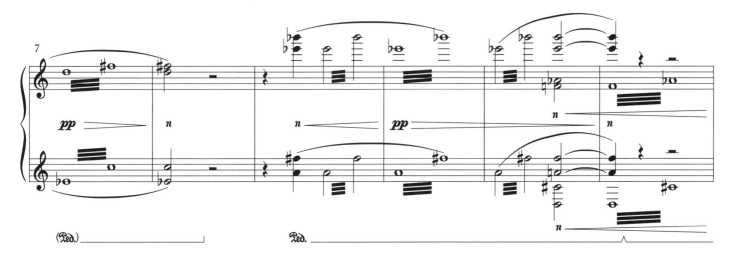

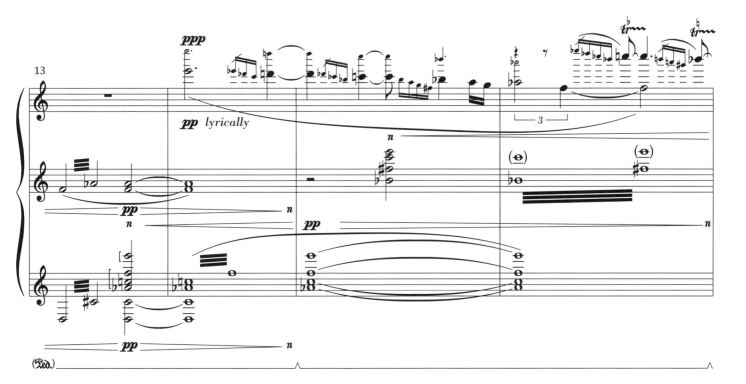

Slightly faster

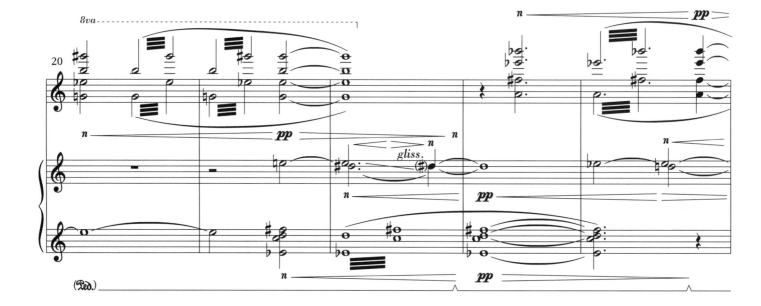

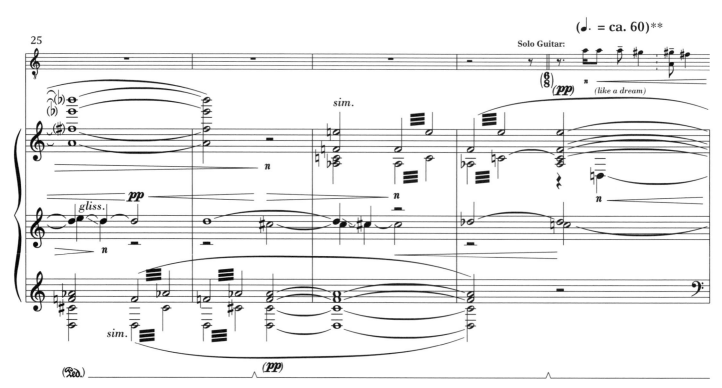

*Repeat pitches freely, as multiple echoes.
**Slightly slower than piano beats.

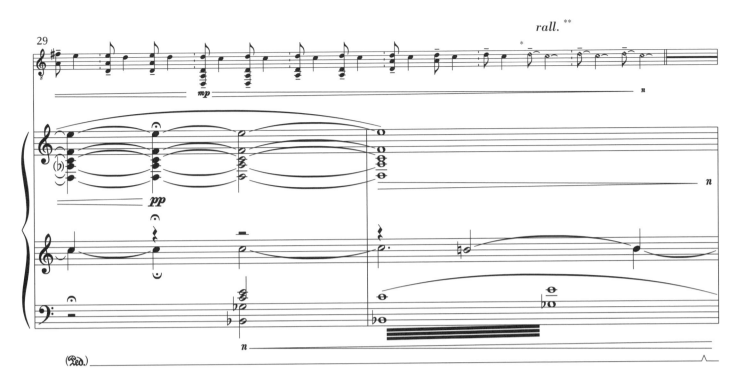

(♩. = ca. 60)

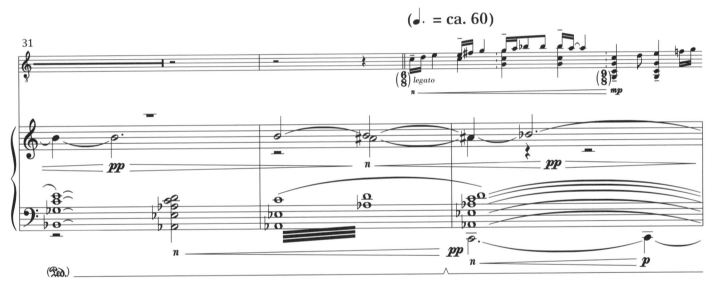

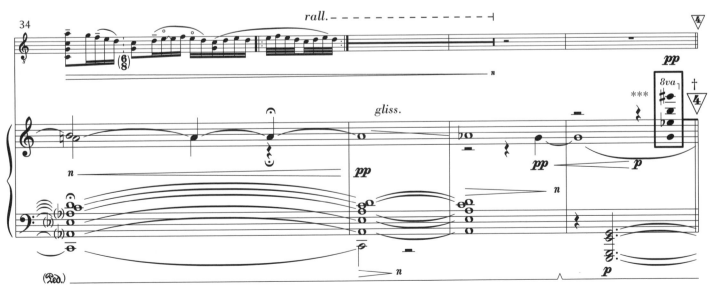

*Guitar harmonics always sound as written.
**Rallentando applies to guitar only.
***Play independent one to five note figures on the indicated pitches, which are to be played like grace note filagrees.
†Free cue beats. The number in the triangle denotes the number of cues. Dashed barlines indicate cue beats.

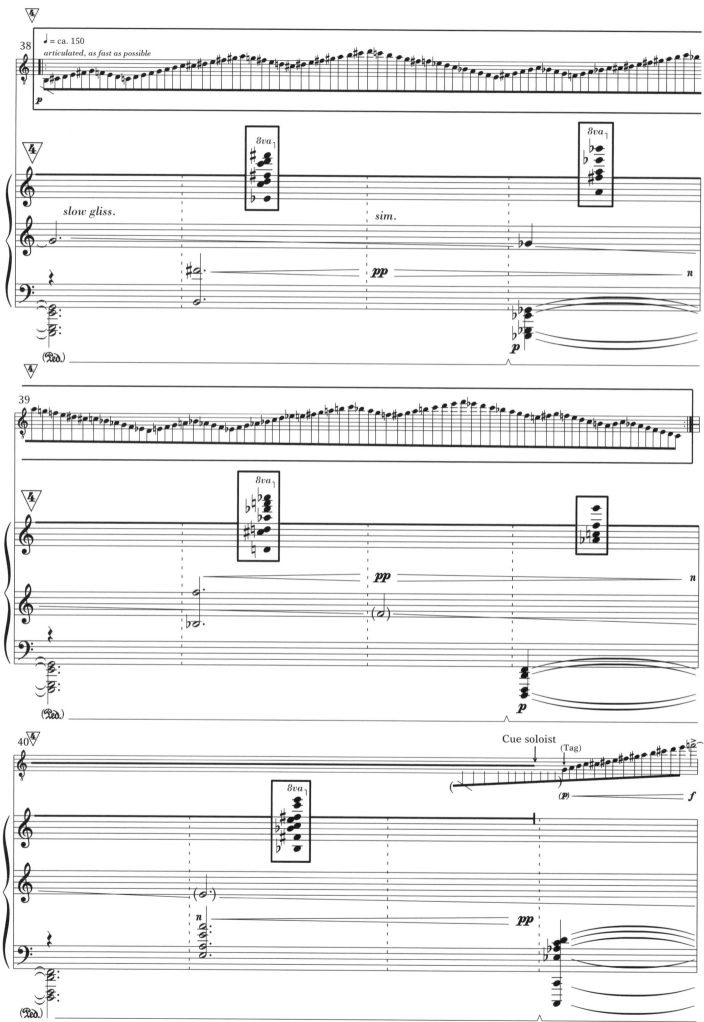

Moving ahead

Lute sound (until bar 71). Play with the tip
of the nail, perpendicular to the string.

Poco meno mosso

*Use fermate only if necessary for realignment.

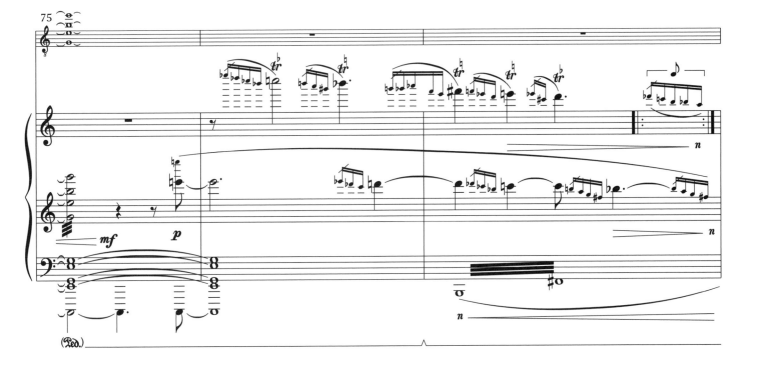

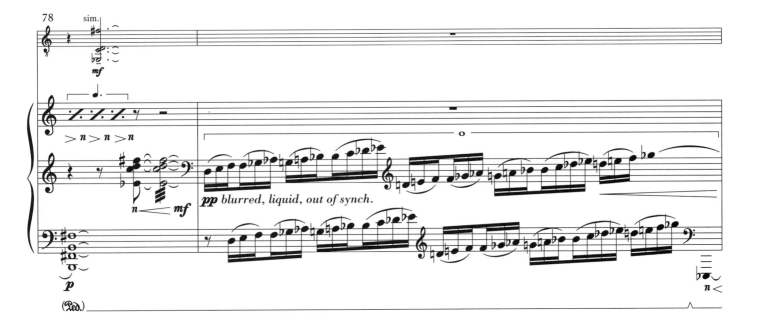

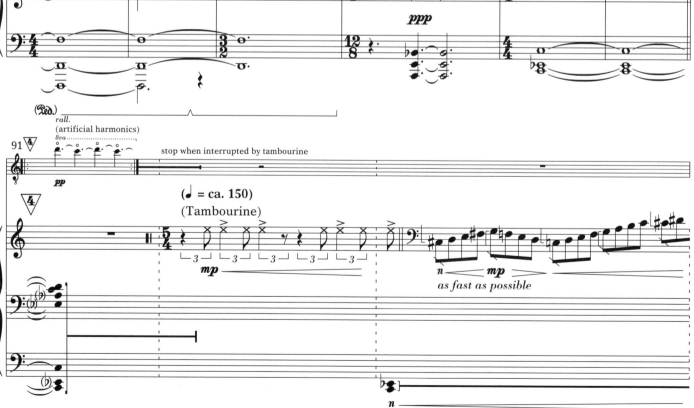

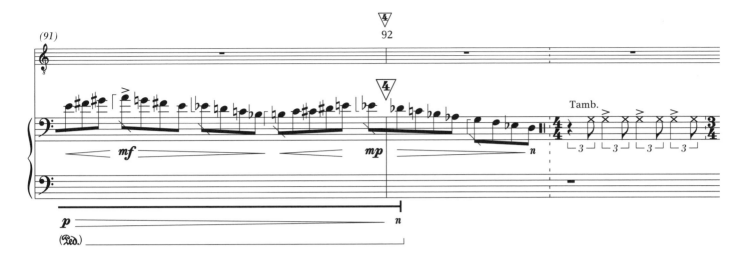
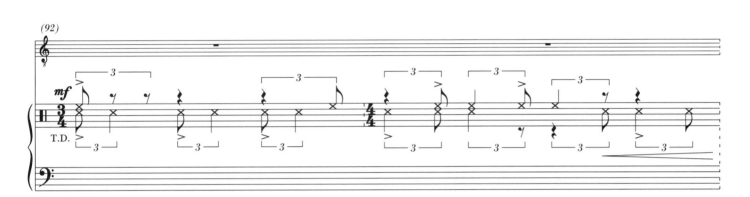

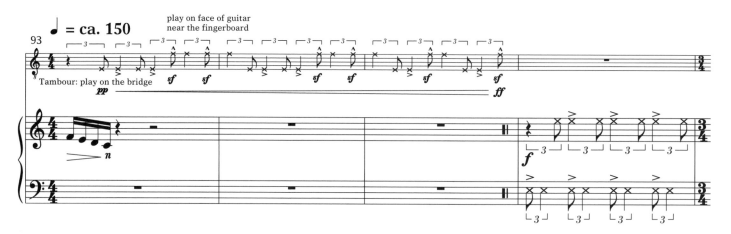

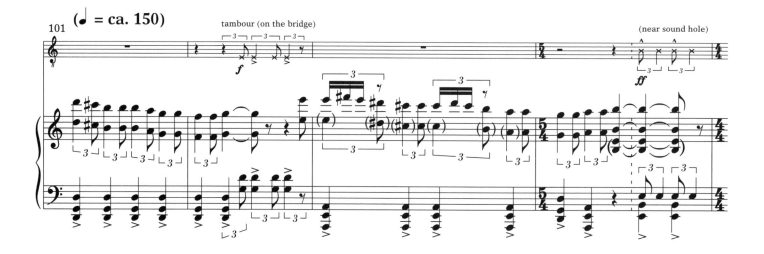

JOHN CORIGLIANO

TROUBADOURS

(VARIATIONS FOR GUITAR AND CHAMBER ORCHESTRA)

Solo Guitar

(fingering by Sharon Isbin)

Performance Note:

If using wireless sound reinforcement, the soloist has the option of entering and exiting from backstage. Begin performance backstage and walk slowly onstage after the opening notes of the run in measure 38. Sit in soloist's chair by fourth cue in measure 40, before tag. At measure 294, walk toward backstage while playing. Measures 309 through the end are performed backstage.

With special thanks to Scott Wilkinson for his assistance.

—Sharon Isbin

ED 4204
First Printing: August 2008

ISBN: 978-0-634-08910-7

G. SCHIRMER, Inc.

DISTRIBUTED BY
HAL•LEONARD®
CORPORATION
7777 W. BLUEMOUND RD. P.O. BOX 13819 MILWAUKEE, WI 53213

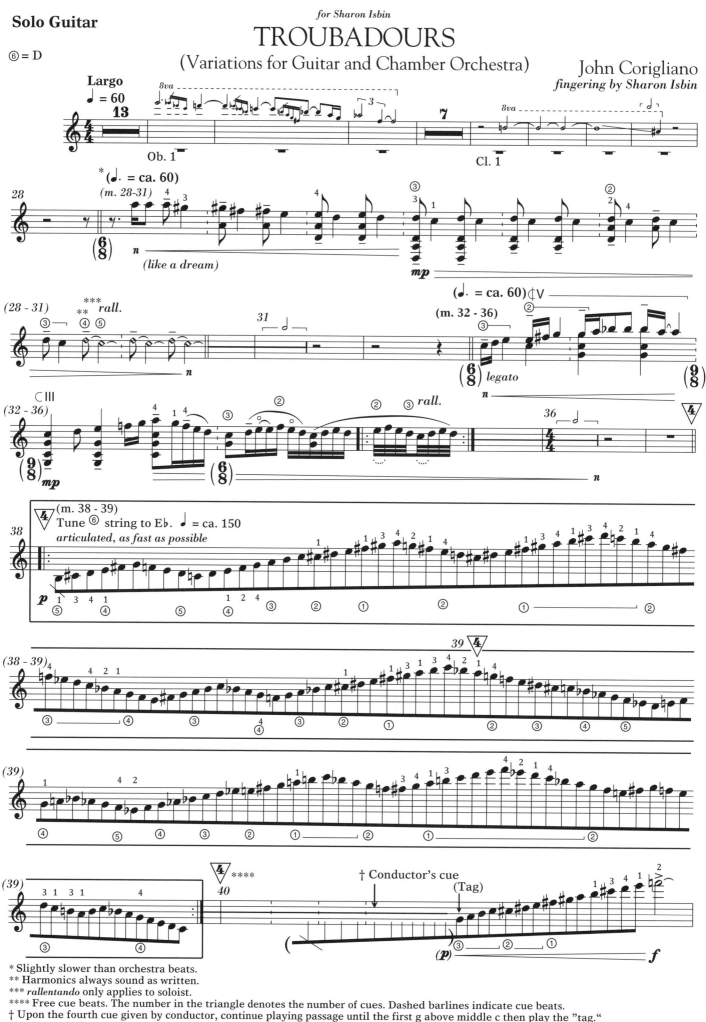

Solo Guitar

for Sharon Isbin

TROUBADOURS
(Variations for Guitar and Chamber Orchestra)

John Corigliano
fingering by Sharon Isbin

* Slightly slower than orchestra beats.
** Harmonics always sound as written.
*** *rallentando* only applies to soloist.
**** Free cue beats. The number in the triangle denotes the number of cues. Dashed barlines indicate cue beats.
† Upon the fourth cue given by conductor, continue playing passage until the first g above middle c then play the "tag."

Achieve bend by pulling E♮ to F♮
releasing to E♮, and bending back to F♮.

A Chantar: La Comtessa Beatriz de Dia

(qu'e - u - sse fait vers lui de - sa - vi - - nen - ce.)

* "X" note heads represent Tambour sounds made by playing in the manner described.

Guitar

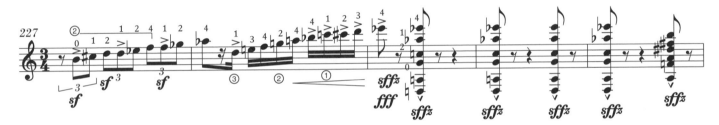

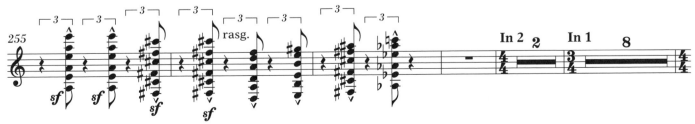

*⑥ string pulled under ⑤ with second finger of l.h. Tuned to produce a note between G♯ and A. Add high A fingered on ④ Play all three strings simultaneously. A "rattling-like" sound will result.

* Use fermata only if needed.

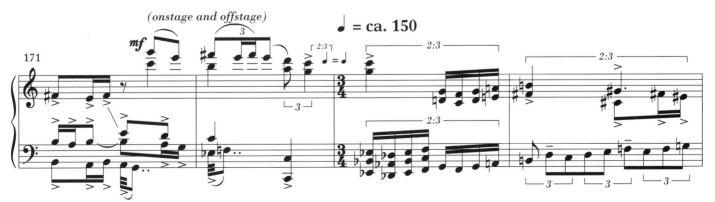

*Sounding dynamics of offstage instruments are in brackets.

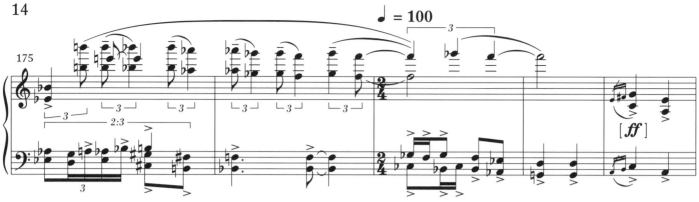

16

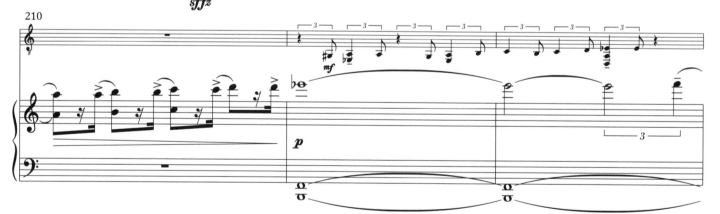

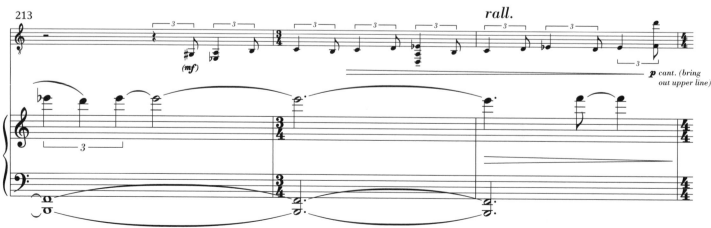

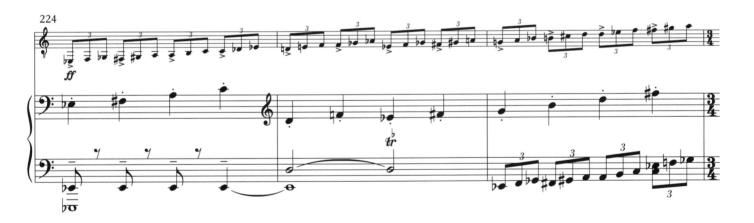

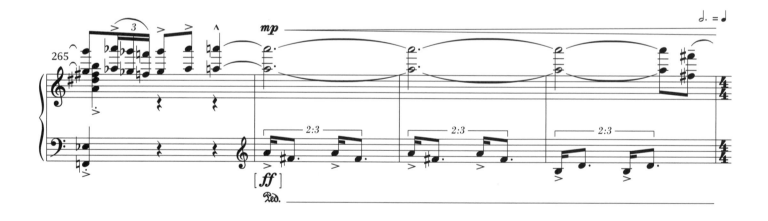

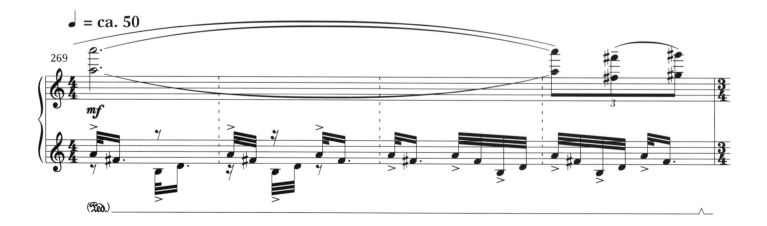

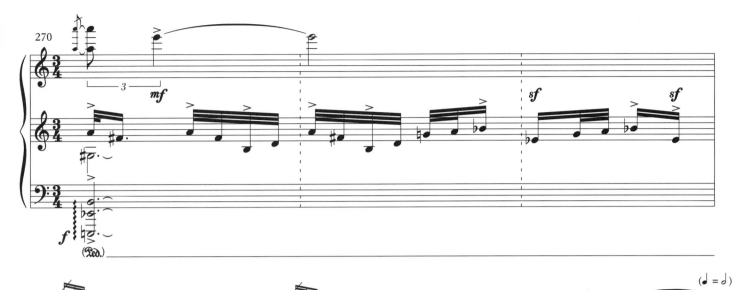

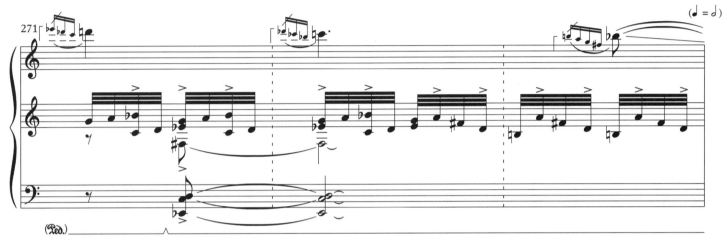

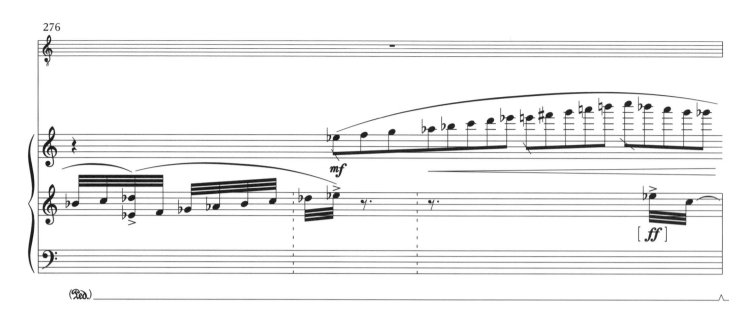

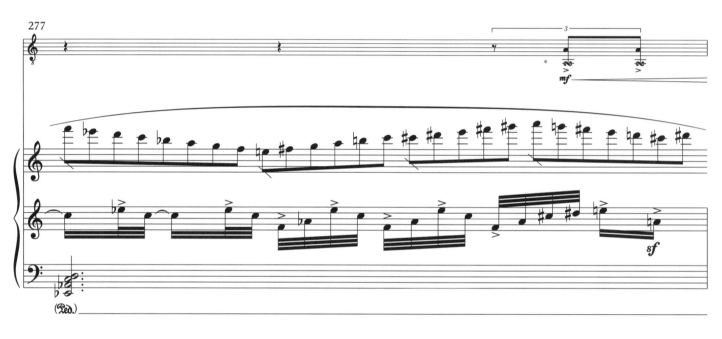

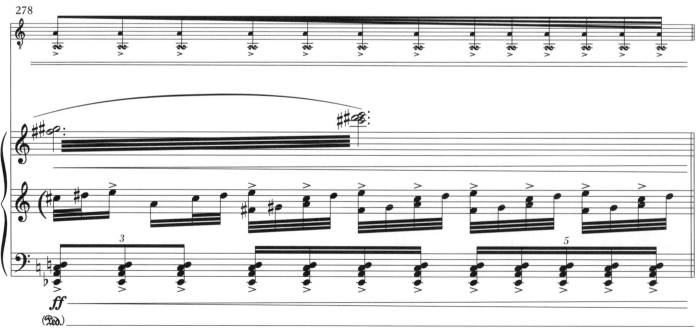

*Pull the E string under the A string with the second finger of the left hand producing a pitch between G♯ and A. Add high A fingered on the D string. Playing the three strings simultaneously will result in a rattling sound.

*Gradually release the E string, producing the A octave between the A and D strings.
** Use fermata only if needed.

Largo ♪ = 60

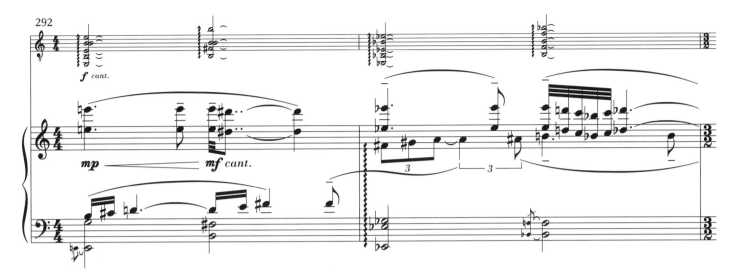

*Use the fermata only if needed.